Reiki
in Everyday Living

*How Universal Energy Is A Natural Part of
Life, Medicine, and Personal Growth*

SECOND EDITION

By:

Earlene F. Gleisner, RN
Reiki Master

white feather press

P.O. BOX 1209 / 43055 HIGHWAY 101 N.
LAYTONVILLE, CA 95454 (707) 984-6048

Reiki in Everyday Living

SECOND EDITION

How Universal Energy is a Natural Part of Life, Medicine, and Personal Growth

by: Earlene Gleisner, RN/Reiki Master

Published by: White Feather Press
POB 1209
Laytonville, CA 95454

Copyright c 1992 by Earlene F. Gleisner
First Edition   First Printing - August, 1992;Second Printing - October, 1993; Third Printing - September, 1994; Fourth Printing - October, 1996
Second Edition - First Printing - July, 2002

Printed in the United State of America

Reference and Quotes of "The Twelve Pathways" are reprinted from Handbook to Higher Consciousness by Ken Keyes, Jr, Fifth Edition, Copyright 1975 by the Living Love Center.
Reference and Quotes of "Namaste" are reprinted with permission from Ram Dass from Grist for the Mill, Copyright 1976 by Unity Press.

Publishers cataloging in Publication Data
Gleisner, Earlene F.
REIKI in Everyday Living: How Universal Energy is a Natural Part of Life, Medicine, and Personal Growth
1. Title   2. Health   3. Therapy, Touch   4. Healing, Self-healing
5. Personal Development

Library of Congress
 Catalog Card Number Pending

ISBN 1-880357-04-6 $13.95 Softcover

This Book is Dedicated to ....

Those of us

who are willing

to touch ourselves

and each other

with love and

with caring hands

October, 1991
Laytonville, CA

3

Reiki in Everyday Living

Table of Contents

Acknowledgments for this Second Edition

Ten years have passed since "Reiki In Everyday Living" entered the world. Every time I reread a section, the thoughts and ideas seem as if I've just read them for the first time. I believe Reiki came through me, whispering the words which needed to be written on paper. This book which desired to be born has been published in Europe, South America, and India and translated into Swedish, Finnish, Portuguese, German, and many other languages I will never know about.

So I acknowledge Reiki, Universal Life Energy, with heartfelt thanks for entering my life and continuing to support my path in this world at this time. I am grateful for having been the vehicle through which this book of inspiration was allowed to pass. I also thank Janeanne Narrin, Reiki Master and author, for suggesting I redo the cover; Carolyn Winters, Reiki Master and friend, for encouraging me to bring out the second edition; and Krista Leamon of The Clayton College of Natural Healing for encouraging me not to let it go out of print because "there's not another one on the market like it."

I hope you will enjoy the new format and the additional essays; "Building Reiki Circles", "Exchanging Energy", and "Trust Reiki" .

I continue to honor and acknowledge every student who has shared themselves in class, all who dare to ask for more in life and from living, and the many who bless themselves daily by struggling through the process of self-realization to learn the art of "being." I especially honor anyone who asks how they may be a part of their own healing and that of our Earth.

"Rakey"

One afternoon in 1977, I was driving on the outskirts of a farming community through freshly-turned fields of earth. My then seven-year-old daughter looked at the regular furrows and called out "Rakey." She said she thought that God had pulled a huge rake through the soil, making "big dents." I looked where her eyes were pointing. Shimmering heat was dancing near undulating ground within the slanted sunlight. I thrilled with the sense of earth's vitality and potential growth. Now that I know the term Reiki as a name for Universal Life Energy in the Usui System of Natural Healing, I continue to hold that spectacle of shimmering vibration as my tangible picture of this energy.

I found Reiki, or rather, Reiki found me.

At the time of my daughter's announcement, I was working as a Registered Nurse in a hospital and growing disillusioned with the bright light/cold steel approach to cures. Rebelling against dehumanizing procedures and treatments, I began my search for more wholeness in health and healing.

In 1984, after many classes, much reading, innumerable life and lifestyle changes, and a Vision Quest, I found Reiki, or rather, Reiki found me.

Since then, time and experience has

deepened and lengthened my understanding of this energy and, because I continue to work at a rural health clinic in various capacities, I am finding more and more methods of application.

A primary theme of this collection of essays and poems is to demystify Reiki so that its effectiveness as a system and as an energy can be documented and accepted as complementary to all systems of health care. A secondary theme is to illustrate how I believe Reiki, when used in everyday living, can increase the quality of life.

Reiki can increase the quality of life.

Realizing there will never be enough words to discuss all there is to know and experience about Reiki, and knowing there are so many ways to connect and reconnect with whatever name you use to behold "life energy," I acknowledge that all the words written here are from my point of view and developed from my own experience.

My hope is that this book will also provide all students and potential students of Reiki with added tools and methods of application. I hope it will increase your excitement over the potential you hold in your hands and will encourage you to use this precious gift with responsibility and respect.

Love and Tantay (Peace),

Earline

What Reiki is

It may seem that Reiki is an intangible, an impossibility in your hand. Something beyond your grasp.

Take heart! What you have experienced in First Degree class has been both an opening and a healing. Reiki is already working in you, on your life and on everything you are touching.

Because each of us is different, I try to minimize, in classes, any attention paid to "hot hands." The focus on this singular type of sensation can be an impediment to your trust. Too often conversation between students becomes a comparison of how hot or cold each others hands are.

Your Reiki experience is uniquely your own.

Your impression of how Reiki comes through you cannot be compared to any one else. Your experience is uniquely your own. Just as unique is your sense of how Reiki feels as it is transferred. There is no place here for competition, because Reiki is not in competition with anything or anybody. Reiki just **IS**. You may feel, see, or sense it as warmth or coolness, light or bright, vibrations or bubbles. Whatever the sensation, it is only important for you to feel when it changes or shifts its expression, so that you will know it is time for you to move your hands to their next position. Whatever sensation you perceive in your hand or your mind is unique to you and the expression of your presence in the world as you relate to it.

Once you've opened to Reiki, you'll never lose it. Some students admit they don't practice Reiki on others or their own bodies, and, *Reiki is forever flowing.* after a while, talk themselves into believing that it has gone away. Reiki, however, is forever flowing. The only thing these students have not been practicing is their attention. They have become unconscious of its flow. Be assured that throughout each day and each night, whenever a need for energy is touched, Reiki will be channeled.

Think now! What is the first instinctive move made when someone is seen in either emotional or physical pain? When a child has pinched a finger or bumped a knee? When an animal is ill? When a tree is broken? What do we do for ourselves when we have an upset stomach or a leg cramp? We reach out and touch the person, our child, an animal, the tree, ourselves.

Reiki is at hand in each of these moments, pulsating toward the need that started it drawing through the vessel of our bodies. Reiki balances and energizes everything in its path, even you and I as it flows through each of us.

Reiki brings about change. These changes are unpredictable and limitless. Thus it is useless for us to set up any kind of expectation around these changes. The healings created may be entirely different than what you or I would expect. We really cannot know what would be best for each other's personhood or our own well-being.

Reiki facilitates changes which are the most appropriate for each of us because it energizes and balances our systems as we each have uniquely created them.

If we can release our judgement and expectation and flow with the balancing and re-energizing changes that occur in our body while reviewing any insight or awareness that enters our minds, Reiki will work wonders on all levels. Damaging patterns of behavior can be recognized and cleared or, at least, more awareness of them can result.

For instance, when I began using Reiki, I became aware of my habit of putting friends into categories and diagnosing their problems in a very clinical fashion. With Reiki, I learned compassion and this defensive barrier to relationships was reduced. I am now enjoying more intimate friendships.

Reiki helps clients become more aware of themselves in new ways.

Reiki helps clients on whom we work become more aware of themselves in new ways. For example, one man who had experienced a painful knee for 13 years had to ask himself why he missed the pain when it disappeared after one full-body session.

Not all clients will be comfortable with these new awarenesses. Some will praise the sense of relaxation and energy directly after a session but discount the entire experience the next day. Others will receive an awareness about diet or relationship problems while on the table, but lose faith in the suggestions when they are called upon to take action. Many will cry or laugh or holler spontaneously. A few will sit up in the middle of the session and say they want to leave.

No matter what occurs, it is best to stand in a place of allowing, for, in this place, there is no expectation and there is no judgement. Here, within each of us, Reiki flows.

It is through each of us that Reiki flows.

For those who will come with their questions, fears, and skepticism, we can ask them to sit or recline comfortably while we gently place our hands on them in the precise manner of the Usui System of Natural Healing. We can ask them to breathe deeply and release their tension while focusing on the pressure of our hands on their body. They may pay attention to any sensations felt in the area under our hands, and/or any sensation in their body.

We might ask them if they feel anything unusual. If they cannot answer, we don't have to try to explain to them what it is they should be feeling. We must let them be. Reiki will create an answer for them in their own experience. We may never know what that is.

It's not up to you or to me to pontificate or recruit anyone into believing in something to which they cannot relate. We are not a religious cult or a movement or an organization which demands all its members believe a certain way.

We are only humans searching to make our world and lives more meaningful, with a little less tension. Friends or clients may prefer massage or Tai Chi, or Karate, or any of the other innumerable ways

14

available to help us understand ourselves and this world.

Reiki may not be for everyone, and yet..............
Reiki will be working in the most surprising ways. We can only show up so as to live our own lives and touch what comes before us.

Very Personally Yours

The only commitment I ask of First Degree students is that they work on themselves and their own healing. This is part of my growing belief that to increase the positiveness of life and have any possibility of creating change for our world, we each must take responsibility for ourselves.

In the beginning of my time with Reiki, I forgot these very teachings of Ms. Takata:

First, heal yourself
Then, your family and friends,
Only then work on others

I came away from my First Degree class ready and willing to heal the world. I offered my hands everywhere until I began to worry: "Why weren't my hands feeling the same as when I had finished the class?" and "Why was I having difficulty focusing on others in a nurturing way?" I became short-tempered with mood swings and very, very tired.

Self-treatment has become my most important tool.

I found myself wondering if Reiki really was the method I had been seeking. I remained concerned until I re-experienced another First Degree class where I saw that I was over-stressing myself past a point of balance where

Reiki could fill me up as I offered my hands to others.

I had not understood that Universal Life Energy pours through our bodies, filling **our** needs **before** it transfers to another person's need. This is what allows us to remain at an even level of energy during multiple sessions for others. **It also means that when we have a more-than-average imbalance in ourselves, physically, mentally, or emotionally, we use Reiki at the same or at a greater rate than our capacity to channel it.**

It became extremely important then for me to focus on my own needs and attitudes so I could return to the "allowing" mode. I learned that I would be less able to be present for another in my best, non-judgmental way if I was so depleted from not having worked on my own issues.

Takata's words resonated in my head:

First, Heal yourself

Thus, self-treatment has become my most important tool.

This can be accomplished by following the same precise system learned in class.

What follows here is an abbreviated outline describing Personal Hand Positions:

HEAD - First Position:
The palms of your hand butt against your cheek bone and your fingers lay across your eyes and your frontal sinuses (forehead). Elbows can be supported o⁄ ˙ʰℯ arms of a chair or pillows if you're sitti⁄ or laying down. You might want tᴄ

pillow between your arms if you're laying on your side.

HEAD - Second Position:
The base of your thumbs and your palms are placed over your ears with fingers pressing the area just over your temples.

HEAD - Third Position:
Your hands can be layered across the back of your head rather than going from the occipital ridge (back of head where nerves from spine enter into the base of the skull) toward your crown

HEAD - Fourth Position (Thyroid):
Place your hands on top of each other at base of your throat.

HEAD - Fifth Position (Thymus):
Place your hands on top of each other on your sternum (breast bone.)

Optional Positions:
Your hands can be placed directly over your ears or over your mouth and chin or across your jaw line.

FRONT:
All positions on the trunk of your body can be reached by placing your right hand on your right side and your left hand on your left side. Starting as high as you want or need, continue down until you can no longer reach

comfortably while reclining.

Your knees and feet are more easily done sitting so you can bring one foot then the other toward you. If this is not possible, the act of applying hands to your inguinal or groin area will be effective.

BACK:

Your neck and shoulders can be reached while sitting in a chair with your arms supported by pillows. A more comfortable position can be accomplished while reclining on your back and moving from one side to the other with pillows supporting your arms.

Your back receives Reiki as your hands travel down the front of your trunk because Reiki transfers from one cell to the next, once the need in the first cell has been met. Thus you treat your front and your back at the same time.

To enhance this process, visualize the 'allowing' of Reiki through your body to the edge of the skin on your back where it touches the material of the chair or the bed. Breathe slowly and evenly.

*   *   *   *

Treating yourself is sometimes hampered by the fact that you may not get clear-cut messages from your hands in areas of need. Shifts in sensations are less easily noticed so you can just move your hands when the hand-positions become tiring. Remember to use breath to assist your relaxation.

19

Of course, Reiki is always at hand for small accidents during the day and when you feel depleted of energy. If you notice early symptoms of a cold, place one or both hands on the Thymus position. This can be done while you are watching tv or driving your car while you steer with the other hand. This helps to boost your immune system.

Reiki is always at hand.

Be aware that your body may very well be sending you a message for rest and more complete attention.

In the tapes and stories we have found of Ms. Takata, we know that she treated herself every morning. She acknowledged herself and brought her energies into balance so she could live her day in fullness. She lived her own words.

I'm asking you to accept Reiki as an integral part of your life too and make it very personally yours.

Reiki and Personal Clarity

Using Reiki on a daily basis can help provide wellness. It is a way in which we can acknowledge our own needs in a healthy way and support our physical well-being. Giving ourselves regular Reiki also acknowledges our personal responsibility for that well-being.

Becoming aware of a general need for the balancing energy of Reiki is not limited to the physical plane. Granted, our physical symptoms are generally the ones to which we pay more close attention. Our physical needs, however, are often dictated by mental, emotional and spiritual ones.

A small burn at the stove or a cut finger or a bumped head are all times when we need a "quick hit" of soothing Reiki.

Daily use of Reiki can provide personal wellness.

The moment these needs occur, I now am learning to stop what I am doing, because I believe something within me has brought my body to this point of injury. I have taught myself to settle into the moment, Reiki my injury, take a deep breath, and ask myself, "OK, what's going on here?"

I usually find that I have been or have become distracted by trying to solve too many issues at one time or by trying to bring more than one project to a successful conclusion. I find that I

21

am worried, or angry, or scattered and not truly focusing on the world around me. Consequently, the world I've bumped into is calling for my attention by helping me to create my personal injury. It's reminding me to "Be Here Now!"

Placing my hand on my injury is an opportunity to assess the situation, reprioritize, reaffirm my commitment to living richly, and resettle into my center.

Reiki strengthens healthy tissue as well as all body defenses.

Sometimes, in that moment, I realize I need to ask for help or to admit to myself I've created a negative attitude. I may simply need 'time out' and can do this by looking through a window or at a favorite corner in my home or having a good laugh at the situation or even a good cry.

Many personal crises express themselves in these small physical injuries, and some are expressed as larger ones. Others may occur in the form of a disease and can range in severity from an acute cold to a chronic illness or specific areas of disease such as tumors.

Concern has been expressed frequently in classes about doing Reiki over these tumors. "Won't the energy cause them to grow bigger?" The answer is that Reiki will assist the body to do what it needs to do to heal itself. You and I cannot know what that will be. In some cases, the tumor does grow larger until it collapses. In other cases, the tumor shrinks. Still in others, there is no physical change at all, but the individual finds increased peace. In a few, the ultimate healing of death arrives quicker.

We must remember in all these cases that Reiki does not nurture illness. Reiki strengthens healthy tissue as well as all body defenses. Reiki brings about balance and embraces each individual's wellness as it needs to be expressed.

Reiki helps each of us begin to listen to our inner voice that is crying out for attention. While using our Reiki hands to strengthen our bodies, we can take time to relax, rest, dream, reassess and reaffirm our beingness. Remember, it is often true: the longer a condition has existed, the longer the time needed for any of us to relinquish it.

Reiki can assist body, mind, and spirit to heal.

Other personal crises are "in the middle of the nighters"! Wakefulness, while meaning anything, can be distressful. Issues abound, for me, at 4AM. In fact, I think someone is awake somewhere at all different times of the night keeping vigil over the frets, frustrations, and issues of the human condition.

As I have watched thoughts and concerns cross my mind in this personal darkness, I have begun to notice different areas of my body experiencing different tensions. I have discovered if I place my hands over the tensed part of my body and breathe as evenly as possible, I can begin to attain relaxation and eventually return to sleep. Sometimes my Reiki hands chase discomfort all over my body for the rest of the night. I either breathe and continue to move my hands from place to place or I do a complete, systematic session. If the distress doesn't go away, I have been known to get up and do journal writing or make lists. Usually, however, I am able to fall back to sleep with my hands in place on some receding strain.

This experience of noting different degrees of tension in different parts of my body has been transformational. I have come to recognize how certain issues cause distinguishably different tensions in different parts of my body.

During the light of day, these degrees of tension can be recognized as responses to all kinds of daily situations. Confrontations, family squabbles or community conflicts bring these about, as well as, emotions or emotional questions, personal insights, or developing spiritual awareness. When these occur, I place my hands on the tense or painful part of my body, and I, literally, hang on.

If I'm in public, this usually assists me in remaining calm while addressing the crisis at hand.

When I'm alone, I am using a technique I've developed to assist me in gaining clarity regarding myself or the situation while letting Reiki nurture my body part. This helps me come to know on a deeper level what is going on. I am calling this technique:

PERSONAL ASSESSMENT PROCESS

One: I Recognize

In this stage, it is enough if I only become aware of the part of my body that is in tension or in pain, and I place my hands there. I am noticing and accepting the message my body is giving me. This can be anything from a sudden dry or sore throat to a cold, headache, a shuddering feeling in an area above my navel and/or an open-hole feeling at the base of my stomach.

Two: I Reveal

Because I accept the belief that emotions can get stuck in cells of the body, I reveal the name of the emotion that is expressing itself as the tension or pain I am feeling as quickly as possible and without judgement.

At one time, a sudden dry throat would always occur just as I was going to speak up on an issue. I discovered when I held the area and quickly named the emotion, it was "Fear." This non-judgmental acknowledgment of emotion has led to a finer discernment of fear, such as fear of failure, fear of success, fear of recognition, fear of challenge. While I am applying Reiki and declaring my emotion, I can tell when I'm in tune with my inner voice because my body will relax with a deep breath.

If I haven't stated the most accurate emotion, I do not experience this relaxing breath. I then encourage myself to try again.

Three: I Explore

Whatever feeling or emotion I have identified in a specific part of my body can have bonded memories that are reinforcing its presence.

These memories are usually from childhood and/or maturing experiences. This is called imprinting. Thus while holding the part of my body which is in tension, I invite a picture to present itself. I begin by looking at what just happened in my immediate present to cause this tension. I then explore my own role and those of others in the present incident. Breathing slowly so that I can remain relaxed, I ask for any corresponding memory from my past.

This step takes trust and practice. It can bring immense understanding of how I repeat lessons until I learn them. It can also illustrate erroneous perceptions from my childhood or left-over emotions from unresolved issues plus help me define an out-grown coping pattern.

Four: I Release

Believing in the theory that recognizing patterns in life and relationships is one important step in making changes, I now bless these moments of clarity. In this way, I am releasing the hold that I feel previous experiences have had on my present life situations.

Breathing slowly again while still holding with my Reiki hands, I feel the pressure/pain reduce. If I have correctly recognized, revealed, and explored the pain, it is released and replaced by the warmth and fullness of Reiki.

These four steps have become a tremendous help in my coping with the challenges and confrontations in my life. They have assisted me in knowing myself and in growing to be more available to others while still being honest with who I am. I acknowledge that this is, of course, not the only way. There are many, many more methods of personal work that can be complemented with Reiki hands, such as journeying, inner child work, repatterning, cognitive behavioral therapy, neuro-linguistic programming, etc. Whatever our inclination or interest, whichever method or personal process

Reiki can help us honor our own process.

we may choose, we can nurture our self-hood, our very being, with Reiki as we work toward greater personal clarity.

Our bodies are the manifestation of our spirit for here and now. It is what we have to work with so that we each can get around and live our lives. Our bodies give us messages regarding our total needs and well-being. When we can learn to honor these messages, we will have another tool so as to keep our human overcoats healthy. Then we can stand in more total balance when we step forward to care for another.

Gifts for the Giver

A Reiki Master can show an individual how to accomplish a total body session and can facilitate an opening and connection with Reiki, but until each individual personally feels his/her own exceptional sense of this energy, there can be difficulty in accepting this process as real.

Any friend or teacher can also point out, suggest, or explain whatever they suppose is our talent or 'specialness'. Inner acceptance of who we each are is what finally helps to develop that inner knowing of our unique talent or 'specialness' in life and gives us that undeniable sense of self. Standing in our center and allowing Reiki to flow through us, getting out of the way of expectation and trusting in the message of our hands are all ways of attaining personal growth and spiritual enhancement. It is also the way of coming to terms with our 'self' and obtaining inner acceptance.

Reiki brings out the genius in each of us.

There is no need for our mind to do anything during a session. Our "being-ness" is enough. This is a form of inner acceptance, of stretching to the very edge of who we are in one small moment and accepting the knowledge, in our heart and head, that this moment is all there is.

Consistent use of Reiki on ourselves and/or others (be that 'other' a tree or an animal or another person) is one way in which to become attuned to who and what we are and to help us become "aware" of other things about ourselves.

As we quietly 'do' Reiki, we slow ourselves down and become more cognizant of feelings, odors, color, taste. We more clearly perceive our physical, mental, and emotional relationships. With this understanding and acceptance, we begin to recognize projects or events or actions we can do. We often discover in ourselves a skill, flair, or knowingness of which we were only marginally aware previously or which was totally non-evident to us. This, then, becomes the genius of ourselves that Ms. Takata said Reiki would bring out in each of us, whatever that genius is.

Now, many of us try to choose the gift or genius that is ours. In this New Age, channeling an alien entity or documenting wisdom-filled words in a book are aspects greatly desired. Or, perhaps, we would like to paint pictures or create inspired stained-glass windows.

These gifts or talents are not impossible. However, the act of saying, "This is what I want to do," may limit all possibilities by focusing on one desired potential.

Learning to release expectation and open to all the possibilities of life can, assist us in the awareness of those exceptional qualities that are ours.

Perhaps we have the skill to listen to another person or to design a better wheelchair. We may be able to paint a wall, grow seed into vegetables, detect a change in weather by our sense of smell, empathize with a friend. The list of possibilities are endless and becoming aware of more than one gift or genius is made possible by accepting the one that comes to us first.

We each can open to the potential of our life.

When we acknowledge that which we do well, we ultimately accept our gift or genius and use it for the benefit of ourselves and everyone around us. Chances are, as we grow in the awareness as a Reiki channel, we will more easily accept our individuality. Then, our capacity of self-awareness will increase, and we will see what else there is for us in our lives. That which we may have desired to do may then be actualized with greater ease and deeper insight than originally envisioned.

Changes

In the quiet practice of Reiki

on plant or animal or self

Spiritual growth increases

inner knowing develops

And our connection

with all things,

grows,

Intensifying a hundred - fold

by the act

of our touching

another.

efg;1990

Reflections

The Reiki advertisement claim I read in the September, 1983 edition of "Common Ground" stated, "You can stimulate your personal and spiritual growth by simply doing a session on yourself or another." I was more than intrigued but also skeptical.

Reiki can stimulate personal and spiritual growth.

In the brochure I received from Rev. Fran Brown, whom I eventually chose as my teacher, I was promised, "Reiki is an impetus to spiritual growth." Although I wasn't born in the "show me" state, I did want to know how and why.

After a few months of using Reiki, I began to experience an openness to new understandings of myself and of my circumstances. It was as if I were viewing life around me differently, as if the window panes of my perception had been washed, or I was able to look at myself through different windows. Reiki was focusing my attention in a new way on myself and my relationships.

I began to develop a sense of belonging, but not to a social group or to an organization. "To what then?" I had to ask myself. The belonging, I'm beginning to believe, was and is to myself and to all that is.

I've pondered this change and talked to many

others who "do" Reiki. We agree that some kind of personal growth work occurs and there is an expansion within our "self" and consciousness while we are practicing Reiki regularly.

That is the "key": practicing Reiki regularly. This can be on our body, our cat or our favorite animal, a tree, or on another human being.

The very idea of allowing our bodies to be a vehicle by which this energy, Reiki, transfers from the Universe to another is an experience in letting go, of standing in our centers and "being". At the same time of this "letting go", we are being totally present so we are aware of our hands and have the experience of feeling the shift in the energy when an area is filled. This shift tells us when to move onto the next area of the body we are working on.

The key is using Reiki regularly.

When I read any of the several books on enlightenment, "letting go" and "living in the present" are the first essential attitudes mandated.

In the 'Handbook to Higher Consciousness - The Science of Happiness' by Ken Keyes, the first three of his Twelve Pathways are categorized under "Freeing Myself" which I interpret as "letting go" and the second three are grouped under "Being Here Now" or "being present".

In 'Grist for the Mill', Ram Dass translates "*Namaste*", a greeting, to mean: "I honor the place in you where the entire universe resides. I honor the place in you of love, of light, of truth, of peace. I honor the place within you where, if you are in that place in you and I am in that place in me, there is only one of us." He continues a little farther in the book; "So that the next time you sit waiting for something to begin you will realize there is nothing that needs to begin, for the beginning, the middle, and the end are already who you are."

When we place our hands on another person in the practice of Reiki, we are actualizing that 'being-ness'; we are standing in the beginning, the middle, and the end. We are freeing ourselves from the tentacles of thought and judgement and settling into our central core. We are joining and becoming one with whatever and whomever we are touching. We are living in the moment, and there is truly "only one of us."

Whenever we do Reiki, we are receiving Reiki too.

The third category of pathways in Ken Keyes' book is "Interacting with Others." Laying hands on another person's clothed or unclothed body is an interaction. When interaction can be done without expectation, it becomes unconditional love. This act can release us from the illusion of separateness that often clouds our minds. The act of laying hands on a tree, a plant, an animal, or any living thing can also release us from isolation and bring us to a new level of openness.

Reading our hands and coming to know when there is a change so we can recognize when to move to the next position becomes a lesson in trusting our inner voice. The fact that we DO move our hands is an experience in taking action based on information from that same voice or inner knowingness. This accomplishes the fourth category of the Twelve Pathways, "Discovering My Conscious Awareness," which states in the 10th path:

"I am continually calming the restless scanning of my rational mind in order to perceive the finer energies that enable me to unitively merge with everything around me."

We are perceiving the finer energies of Reiki and "merging with everything" during a session.

Reiki can be a catalyst.

It is amazing to understand that the very simple act of performing a Reiki session is intrinsically tied into the lessons of spiritual growth:

* releasing the events of life and allowing the sensation of Reiki to flow through body, mind, and spirit;

* being conscious of the 'here and now'

* coming into interaction with another through the laying-on-of-hands without expectation but purely out of love

* listening and trusting and taking action on any awareness that occurs during a session.

Simply put, the practice of Reiki is a catalyst for expanding our awareness of ourselves, our work, and our spiritual growth while making stronger our connection with all that is.

Building Reiki Circles

Many of us who have been opened to Reiki have a natural urge to offer this energy to family and friends. Sometimes we forget our need to experience the benefits of Reiki under the hands of others.

Sharing Reiki regularly with others builds community.

Gathering together Reiki people, whether they do the 'work' professionally or privately, whether they are First or Second Degree or Master level, or whether they were even trained by our same Master, can be rewarding as well as challenging.

As a First Degree student in1984, I knew of only two other people, in my small town, who practiced the Usui System of Natural Healing, and they preferred to only work on family and friends. Because my goal was to spread the word about Reiki, I invited my Master several times to teach others this simple hands-on healing tool. After two years, there were twenty others initiated into this system.

Natural enthusiasm occurred in our three day Reiki class where each set of hand positions were practiced by all students. This enthusiasm formed a natural bridge between the class experience and forming a Reiki Circle which met on a regular basis.

As we came together, we developed the

following basic agreements:

(1) We agreed to come to six meetings in a row and scheduled these every other week for the first set then eventually stretched the times to monthly.

(2) We honored the individual on the table by not chatting about our personal lives or processes.

(3) Whoever was sitting at the head during the first treatment was the next individual on the table. This process assisted all of us in not having to make a decision as to who was next because we all rotated clockwise around the table. This also assisted us in not staying in one place for several rotations.

Respecting each other is a gift inspired by Reiki.

(4) Up to eight people could work on one individual at a time: one at the head and one at the feet, two facing each other over the chest, two facing each other over the abdomen. If two more arrived, they were moved in to help at the knees. The application of Reiki was completed on one side when all had felt the slowing of the draw of Reiki into the person on the table. We decided to work with more people at one table instead of dividing up so as to be able to assist more people in a short amount of time.

(5) If someone wished to sit out a round, after receiving Reiki, we offered them that space

(6) Snacky, light foods with juices and teas were brought for treats during the circle and were available all afternoon or evening, especially between individual applications.

(7) Anyone had the right to ask that a

particular hand position not be used or a specific body area not be touched.

(8) Anyone had the opportunity to ask that a certain area be touched, if it was not usually included in the overall application

Openness is important for a successful Reiki circle.

(9) We agreed to refrain from commenting on the 'degree of draw' in order to prevent any individual from fixating on the idea that something was wrong. We invited individuals to tell us what they felt afterwards.

(10) Each person was offered pillows under their knees or head so as to make them as comfortable as possible.

(11) Soothing music was often softly playing in the background.

(12) The length of time of our coming together was always agreed upon and always negotiable when the time for closure neared.

Sometimes we found there were enough volunteers to rotate the location where we joined together for shared Reiki application. Sometimes one home became the focal point of this Circle.

Two decisions had to be made and remade on a regular basis. Did we want to invite those who had not yet taken the First Degree Class and/or those who had learned Reiki from a Master other than myself or Fran Brown? Most of the time, the Circle decided to share Reiki only with those who had participated in classes. They felt they wanted to continue supporting the bond of trust and openness which had developed between them.

When the circle has been in my home, I have asked if the group minded working on someone who has not yet taken the class. I like to offer a 'one time' visit and with only one new person invited per gathering. I don't do this without the agreement of the group, however. I also encourage these individuals to learn Reiki and join the group. If they wish only to receive, I ask them to become a client of any one in the group who is offering Reiki as a practitioner.

Reiki Circle is not a time for competition

At times, we have agreed to welcome those who have learned Reiki from another Master. I hold the vision for all that this is a time of sharing Reiki, not a teaching time, but a personal healing time. If anyone wishes to compare notes on different methods learned or different tools developed, I invite them to talk to me directly or to others in the group either before or after the Circle. I've heard some interesting differences that would divert the attention of our healing intent if they had been brought into the Circle.

We always begin our Circle with a one word check-in of our feelings at that moment and a prayer that we will join together as one to benefit all. We may also draw an Angel Card as a focus for contemplation during the Circle.

We close with a brief description of any shift we might have felt during our time together. I do like to suggest that we offer Reiki to our Mother Earth or any hot spot internationally which the group feels they want to focus on. We use the method developed by Mary McFaddon in her Reiki Outreach

International Project.

Our Circle contracts and expands in number depending on the season, the weather, and what is going on for each of us. It's like a living, breathing organism in its own way. Sometimes we've agreed not to come together for over a year and then we begin again.

Group offerings of Reiki to world situations can bring about change.

As the world-wide Reiki community grows, our circles are creating focal points of healing in all the countries of the world. Many of us have also connected with others over the Internet and join together at specific times to send Reiki all over the globe. Holding the sense that we are offering Reiki to the highest good of all matter can help us release fear and stand in the perfect moment that is the light and love of this all encompassing energy.

Exchanging Energy

"I've got a big problem about charging anybody for Reiki, especially my family and friends. I think it should always be free."

"You know my friend wanted to give me something for the Reiki session I gave her last week but I told her she already had given me something by letting me practice on her."

What is the value of something for nothing?

How many times these issues of payment and practice come up for me and for students. In my heart of hearts, I am so grateful for the ability to offer my hands in a way that might relieve someone's pain or anxiety. Yet, I can find myself counting the dollars from a cash-paying client and planning the payment of a long standing bill.

Ms. Takata's stories addressing these issues have been retold in books regarding her life and her teachings. I remember her tale about Dr. Mikao Usui working the slums of Tokyo. He was disappointed at recognizing returning beggars who had been physically healed. He realized they had placed no value on their healing nor on his offering of healing in the first place. They had no desire to 'give back' or of even working for a living. This is when, we are told, he developed the Five Precepts

41

and instituted the idea of the exchange of energy for healing sessions.

Ms. Takata tells the story on herself of how she went against the warning of her teacher, Dr. Hayashi, not to give Reiki away. She taught Reiki to friends who had helped her when she was sick. But, when one or the other had a sick or injured child, they still brought the child to Ms. Takata for treatment. When she asked, "Why didn't you give Reiki?"

The bounty from Reiki is immeasurable.

They answered, "Oh, you are the real healer."

In the process of her giving the teaching of Reiki away, they had not been given the opportunity to place their own value on what they had received.

Surely for our close family, when a child has a pinched finger, or a husband has had surgery or our mother splashes boiling water on her hands, we offer Reiki without a thought of reimbursement. These instances are often the very basic reason we took Reiki in the first place. We just wanted to feel we could do something. We just wanted to be able to help and to relieve some of our own anxiety.

I've been rewarded by my family members in these instances when my husband finished cooking dinner while I held my son's pinched fingers, or when my husband walked sooner than the doctors expected and he was able to begin sharing chores again. I was blessed by my mother's wondrous look at the difference between her unblistered hand where I had Reikied it and her other unReikied hand where two large blisters had formed.

For those outside my close family, I often offer my hands to co-workers as they sit at their computers, or for a sprained ankle or other minor problem. When someone is in the hospital, I will sit and hold their hand or foot, knowing that every little bit of Reiki they can receive will help.

When someone asks to experience Reiki, I often give them a session for their birthday or I've employed any number of transitional methods to move the individual and myself into a relationship based on a more formal exchange of energy.

These methods have evolved from my having sat with these issues of when and how much to 'charge','accept', 'allow', etc. for many years.

Here in my hometown, a Reiki Master of a different school of thought would give the first Reiki attunement to clients during their treatment session. Once a month, she would then gather any interested clients together for classes and give the remaining attunements for free, even Second Degree and her division of Master level into two levels. She often stated, "Reiki is of the spirit and therefore cannot be priced."

Honoring Reiki brings a greater degree of connection to its potential.

A year later one of her students who was creating a massage therapy practice complained, "You can't even give Reiki away anymore." I had to agree with her since I was closing my own office for lack of clients. No one wanted 'just Reiki'.

One part of the answer regarding energy exchange, of course, is around how we each view money and potential and abundance. I understand

43

these themes in my life much better now. Actually, I've finally come to realize that the answers to these energy exchange issues are not about me but are part of a bigger question regarding my relationship with the person who is receiving Reiki. I began to sort things out by asking myself the following questions:

(1) How am I respecting myself and the commitment I've made to my clients as an open channel for Universal Life Energy?

(2) Am I taking away from my client's opportunity to express their intention to be healed by my not accepting payment?

(3) In my relationship to clients, by not allowing payment to me as the practitioner, am I keeping them beholden to me? What is my motive in doing this?

(4) What is it about my trust in this healing technique? Why is it that I am not allowing others to show value for it too?

(5) What is my ultimate purpose in not expecting an exchange of energy?

Our clients' opportunities to acknowledge their own healing is more of a process for them than it is for me to receive anything.

Watch the movement of the energy when someone gives and receives. A space is created as that individual opens a part of themselves to the potential of receiving through the act of 'giving away'. Whether a client brings canned stewed tomatoes, fresh baked bread, beaded earrings, or cash, they are making a statement of their own intent to be open to the energy of healing. It is not wise of us to stop that flow.

As to the thought that someone is only practicing Reiki after a First Degree class, that thought needs to be cast away. There is no such thing as practicing the channeling of energy, we just are. However, what we might feel we are practicing is the hand positions or trying to define the shifts and changes of energy under Reiki hands. This can be considered the learning curve of Reiki. For this reason, I like to have my students consider that they are not practicing, only gathering information.

Offering Reiki is something we can do for the rest of our lives, no matter what level of class we've completed. One does not need to go any further than First Degree training so as to be able to offer healing energy for themselves and others.

You can't practice Reiki. Reiki just is.

If a formal, professional, Reiki practice is begun, then the issue of exchanging energy becomes a real consideration and a belief in self-worth, Reiki, and concept of money will be challenged.

For years, I charged $25 per Reiki session in our small community because of the depressed logging economy. It served as a standard of exchange for helpful hands in my garden or office, jam and syrup, and many other creative items as well as checks and cash. After a time I shifted to accepting payment based on what a session was felt to be worth to each client. I was totally surprised one day when a woman said, "I can't pay you enough."

As she handed me a hundred dollar bill, she added, "You just saved my life."

Spiritual Precepts of Reiki

Just for Today...

Do Not Anger

Just for Today...

Do not Worry

Honor your parents,

teachers, and elders

Earn your living honestly

Show gratitude to all

living beings.

The Spiritual Precepts

In the beginning of my experience with Reiki, I had a grudging belief that attention to the Precepts would be of assistance to me.

The origins of the Precepts continue to be clouded by the creativity of our oral-history tradition. Wording is shaded differently by many Masters who teach. I now have seen and heard the Precepts presented in many different ways and have come to understand that it is in the original wording by Takata that these guides retain their most value to me. Viewed in the context of her phrasing, they represent attitudes toward life.

On a taped recording of a class given before she made her transition, Ms. Hawayo Takata, the Reiki Master who brought these teachings to the western world from 1940 to 1980, listed the Precepts in the following manner:

1. Just for Today, Do Not Anger

2. Just for Today, Do Not Worry

3. We must count our blessings and honor our fathers and mothers, and our teachers and neighbors and honor our food by making no waste and show gratitude for all this also.

4. Make your living honestly

5. Be kind to everything that has life.

There has been much discussion and disagreement regarding the origins of these Precepts. Some believe they are based on the Meji Emperor's Five Rules of Life and are Shinto in origin. Others believe these writings correspond as antidotes to the Five Hinderances to spiritual growth and enlightenment as detailed by Buddha in his teachings at Deer Pond.

Whatever their source of inspiration for Dr. Usui, I can now see them more clearly as positive influences on my life and learning. When I work with them as intentions, I find that I am much more open to the abundance of Reiki and of life.

As a wife and mother, worry was the first Precept I began to work on. Worry was a habit for me, I discovered, as it seems to be for most of society.

The Precepts are "be here now" tools.

Pick a subject! Any subject! I bet that either you or I can find at least one detail in that subject that can act as a source for worry. Have you ever given attention to what happens in your body or in your life when you begin to worry about something in the past, present, or future?

Try this. For just a moment, focus on one of your worry items and pay attention to how your body feels.

Mine feels as if all the cells have huddled together, clinging to each other, allowing no space between them. I feel closed in on myself, unable to see into the world around me. The words "Threat" and "Fear" enter my brain and twist around and through my consciousness leaving no room for other thoughts, let alone other possibilities.

Worry can be fear on the inside.

Worry has pushed everything else out of the way and has closed me off from what is happening outside. The act of worrying has the side effect of closing me off from the source of Reiki and shutting me down as a channel.

As I see it, if worry is the internalization of Fear, then Anger is the externalization of it.

Now choose a topic of anger and feel your body again.

Mine feels as if all the cells have been dammed up and are reservoirs of blood and held breaths and screams. My cells feel engorged and pushed so close together, there is no space between them. I feel tight inside and every part of me is shaking with tension.

Again, I feel stuck, shut down. Only when I choose to relinquish the total involvement with either of these emotions do I feel my breath flow in and out and recognize my openness to Reiki and to life.

In a story about anger, Ms. Takata shared her learning experience about this Precept with several of her students. On her return boat trip from Japan, her cabin mate had been in need of money and Ms. Takata had cheerfully helped her. This woman, however, continued to return again and again for more help, making promises to return the money she had borrowed but then breaking her promises. Ms. Takata admitted she was becoming furious but, because she was trying to live by the Precepts, she continued to recount the good points of this woman and to assist her without anger.

Dr. Hayashi came to Hawaii at her request and began traveling with her to help create and teach classes as a Reiki Master. At her wits end, she finally told Dr. Hayashi about the situation, admitted her anger, and asked what she could do.

Anger can be fear on the outside.

He apparently shook his head at her and said, "The Precepts only say, Do Not Anger. They do NOT say never to DO anything about it."

Later, when Ms. Takata saw the woman in question walking toward her house, she met her on the porch. Before the woman could speak, Ms. Takata pointed to the steps of the porch, "See those steps?" she asked. "They go both ways. Please go down them and never come back!"

These two statements, Do Not Anger and Do Not Worry, are not asking us to stuff our emotions or push them away so as not to acknowledge them. These Precepts of Reiki invite us to look at our emotions, investigate the sources of their hold on us, and thread our way toward the realization of their origins. In this way we may be able to acknowledge their presence and do something about them before they constrict our lives.

When I discovered that worry and anger were versions of fear, I began a dialogue with myself about my personal fears by asking what was the worst possible thing that could happen to me around any feared situation. Once I've developed an answer, I ask myself if there is any action I can take to move away from this outcome, or if I can live with this possibility.

I allow this feeling of fear to become a "sign post" which simply tells me to review a situation. I am more able to feel and deal with my emotions and ultimately relinquish them by logically dealing with the various situations which inspired the feelings. I find I am relieved of the burden of constantly worrying about an event or a circumstance or of becoming angry at it. I feel I have learned how to "get out of the way" of the situations of my life and move on.

I am more able to move past each crisis with fewer incapacitating moments of emotion and with more honest sensations of feeling. For the most part, anger and fear are no longer constricting my life or my attention or, more importantly, the flow of Reiki.

Fear can constrict the flow of Reiki.

The third Precept has many component parts when taken the way Takata last stated them. Honoring those who teach us, not only our parents, but all teachers, can bring honor to ourselves. It can strengthen our ties to our origins and give us some concept of where we've come from. When we also honor those who are part of our lineage as Reiki practitioners, we can then strengthen our tie to the passage of this energy.

Honoring our food is more than being grateful for the bounty of our lives. What we choose to feed our minds, our bodies, and our spirits is a statement of how we wish to grow and how we honor ourselves.

Making no waste is asking that we know how much we need to use, how much we are willing to share, and how well we are taking care of what we have. There is no waste when we also compost and recycle. All is used and honored and makes great sense in this day and age of hunger, homelessness, and contamination.

"Show gratitude for all this also" refers not just to food and teachers, but to all experiences, blessings, and opportunities that make up our lives.

When I forget to show gratitude or acknowledge compliments or a rewarding experience, etc., I lose track of them and they are not sealed into my consciousness. If I do that often enough, I find I lose a sense of the bounty of my life and tend to get a little depressed.

Gratitude affirms Abundance.

Counting my blessings then becomes a way to turn my attention around to a more positive frame of reference. Consciously showing gratitude seems to bring more things to mind for which to be grateful. It teaches me to allow myself to receive and affirms my connection with the abundance of the Universe. Separateness disappears and I feel at one with all things.

The next Precept of "Make Your Living Honestly" speaks on two levels: (1) Making the effort to earn a living, and (2) Doing it in a fashion which acknowledges abundance and potential.

Creating a business, digging a ditch, painting a picture, for instance, are each efforts by individuals to establish a focus for personal expression. This action helps to create a bond with life and opens a pathway to receivership so that the honor of payment is also created. This may be in the form of money, bartered goods, or self-reward. This is also showing personal responsibility for taking care of one's self and one's needs.

When we can accomplish our livelihood to the best of our ability and with honesty, we can be open and more able to attract honesty in others and draw prosperity to ourselves.

Honest work creates a positive focus.

Thus, not creating a job or not doing it honestly creates feelings of deprivation and desperation. These feelings can often lead to such negative actions as theft and lies. These negativisms can close down our channel.

The final Precept, "Being Kind to Every Living Thing," reminds me that I am not alone, that I am a part of the whole of the living universe, and that I am not above or below anything or anyone else. This reminds me that we are all equal and puts me in touch with the living essence of energy that flows through all beings and things, be it a tree or a flower or an animal. Even the elements of the earth that have become chemicals and form plastics or rugs have energy. I am more able to understand the philosophy of the American Indian,"All that casts a shadow has spirit."

When I read these Precepts to a new class, I read them more slowly now. I find they embody an element of reason and reassurance in their wording that helps me remember I can do no more than live this day. The flow of words suggests I always have another chance. If I lose my conscious intent and become angry or worried or wasteful or if I forget that I am a part of all that is, I will always have the

_____ opportunity to try again.

Reiki is 'from' and 'for' all life.

Because these five statements are more like guides or suggestions, the responsibility for incorporating them into our lives rests solely within each of us. We are gently asked to become our own center with the Precepts of Reiki acting as the next steps to our spiritual growth, to our emotional maturity, mental clarity, and ultimately, to our total well-being.

Different Decisions

What do others do
>When there's no one there to love?
>>Do they run with freedom
>>>or with fear?
>>Do they cry or laugh?
>>>Play solitaire?
>My heart hardens a little!

What do others do
>When there's no place, anywhere
>>for peace?
>>Do they stride
>>>with steady pace
>>>through their lives?
>>Or stumble?
>>Do they scream?
>>>Or adjust?
>My soul dies a little!

What do others do
>When there's no one to give them
>>love?
>>Do they run from another to
>>>another?
>>Reaching at all who turn away?
>>Do they touch more
>>>and feel less?
>>Or walk in the sun alone?
>I eat too much!

efg;1976

A Lifetime of Decisions

This experience we call life is filled to the brim with decisions. During every waking moment, we are faced with more choices than we can possibly comprehend.

We are often semi- or un-conscious of the threads of life we spin with each thought or direction of thought our minds take. Some decisions are merely reactionary; some are carefully and methodically made. Some major resolutions are brought about by a culmination of seemingly inconsequential decisions with small conclusions intertwined in their process.

One growing realization of mine stands out here: my decisions today are affected greatly by the choices I made yesterday.

As an example, to be able to decide what to have for dinner, I must take into consideration what I decided to buy at the store. I had to choose a day to go shopping in the first place. I also had to consider what my family would eat based on recipe-searching and preparation and individual likes and dislikes of each one of them, plus my knowledge of who is on a special diet and what all of our schedules are for the day and the week. Adding further to the background of the choice, while

Yesterday's choices effect today's experiences.

shopping, I had to have figured out how much money I had to spend and, initially, choose a method of earning money so I could spend it.

The point I'm trying to make here is that I have brought to this particular decision, as I do to every one of my decisions, the entirety of my past experience. I have brought my understanding of who I am and what I can accomplish in a given period of time, my known likes and dislikes as of this moment, my understanding of those I live with, and my projection of who I am or want to be in the future along with what my goals are for today, next year, and so forth.

All that we are, or aren't, is a result of our choices.

All that we are and have experienced is embodied in every single decision we make and each decision creates a new experience. Until we make any decision, we have no real idea of what the experience will be. Thus, we never really make mistakes; we only create experiences we either like or dislike.

The only difficult part of this concept is agreeing to the facts that (1) each of us is really free to make any choice we want and (2) we can create change by choosing to do so.

As a teen-ager I decided to believe that smoking cigarettes looked grown-up and that I liked the buzz they gave my head. At that time, I chose to smoke and built a 2 plus pack-a-day habit for 22 years. I enjoyed the experience until at the age of 38 I began to notice the burn holes in my clothes, the cigarette droppings at the table, my shortness of breath, and a morning cough. For these and more reasons, several years ago, I finally was able, after five unsuccessful attempts, to put them aside. Multidimensional excuses, personal views of myself and my world, plus my attitudes had to be confronted before I could accomplish my liberation from this habit. Cigarettes had become an integral part of my relationship to myself and to the world around me.

Reiki can support changes in our and other's choices.

I had to look at what I was gaining, what was my payoff, the emotions involved, and the history I had with my initial decision to take up this habit. I had to rethink each previous decision that had created my dependency on nicotine. With journal work, I discovered I didn't feel I deserved to take a break from work unless I called it a "cig break". In tense situations, I thought I needed a cigarette to calm my thoughts. The former decision had to do with my self-image, the second had to do with smoke-screening my feelings. These were views of myself I had created by choice.

Thus, I challenged myself to create a new self-image by making new decisions. It wasn't just an intellectual exercise. It was filled with fear, anxiety, sadness, and anger. Each emotional experience was supported with my Reiki hands and with each new decision, I was able to rebuild a "me" who could make the "change of mind" necessary to live without smoking. I also have to accept the fact that twenty-two years of smoking left me with a decreased ability to breathe on exertion. My teeth are brittle from the years of hot fumes passing over them.

I'm not attempting, here, to lecture on the evils of smoking. I am using my experience simply to illustrate how my decisions affected my life and breath. These decisions led me to experiences I did not like and brought me into a situation which is still greatly affecting the quality of my life.

Ultimately, all decisions direct our lives as to whether or not we are going to get sick with certain diseases, and to a degree, whether we are going to place ourselves in positions that could lead to accidents, or be in environments where catastrophes can happen.

It is very difficult to accept that our choices are responsible for whatever happens to our body. No one wants to believe that he or she might have chosen their car accident or their cancer, or be responsible in any way for any upsetting incident in their life. In fact, the realization of this responsibility is invariably painful. But it is this very understanding that can help to explain the intricacies of the healing process.

Do regular and consistent Reiki on chronically ill clients.

Whatever our background or experience in health or in healing, it's important to begin to understand this complexity. Just as one decision builds on another to create disharmony, disease, etc, we can build a new set of choices which will determine to what degree we have chosen to be healed. Ms. Takata's advice was to do regular and consistent Reiki sessions for a chronically ill patient. Consecutive Reiki sessions give the body, mind, emotions, and the spirit a chance to come together in a relaxed and energized state. A chance, as it were, for a person to rethink individual and collective decisions on some (or every) level. An opportunity, in the quiet, for someone to sort through past selections and experiences. All of this can occur without the practitioner or even a client being aware that it's happening.

Reiki supports decisions for change.

I believe that what we see as "miraculous healings" are actually the coming together of this energy, Reiki, which facilitates the rebalancing of a total being, and any individual who has decided on all levels to accept and hold onto that balance. For some persons, this moment can be instantaneous, and a miracle is announced. We hear and read of these frequently. For most of us, the degree of rebalancing comes steadily or in small increments, and this is what we usually see in ourselves and in our Reiki practices.

On some occasions, we will see a transformation during one session, but then a gradual return to the original problem. The body might have been willing, but the emotions or thoughts or attitudes were not ready for the change.

Just as it is with any decision to create a new experience, we cannot know what the experience is until we make the decision to do it. Any movement from one habit or view of life to another cannot be known to its fullest extent until we decide to do it and accomplish it.

To continue with my personal example, I could not have realized that setting tobacco aside would change the pattern of my marriage relationship or open up a new challenge of self-discovery around co-dependency. I had no idea that it would increase my dislike for certain odors. I decided to return to smoking several times until I had made decisions as to how to deal with these and other challenges. My Reiki hands on my body's areas of tension helped me remain calm enough to work through these situations.

Using Reiki teaches us to stand without judgement or expectations.

Thus, Reiki helps us recognize our opportunities to make any choice or decision we wish.

Remember always, just as this decision to create disease is personal, so is the decision to create health. Each person will do it in their own way. Some of us may decided as we are expected to. Others of us may make the ultimate healing decision to let loose of this life experience.

Keep in mind, then, that as practitioners or for ourselves, we are only present to facilitate the decision-making process by channeling Reiki and being present without judgement.

Space and Permission

Have you ever noticed how individuals take their places in waiting areas or classrooms where there are plenty of seats? Commonly a person will sit with an empty seat on either side. If the entire room becomes crowded, most people will keep their places. At other times, if the vacant seats are filled, some individuals will leave.

Have you ever watched two people in conversation? One leans forward to emphasize a point and the other backs away. When the first returns to their original stance, the second one returns also. In effect, a consistent yardage has been maintained between their bodies.

Every life form has a comfort zone.

When I began to notice this happening to me, I initially worried about body odor or possible bad breath. Then, in a communications seminar, I became aware of this concept of personal space.

Theories and descriptions vary in their interpretation. Some authorities believe there is an area at the edge of the skin which is charged by the presence of an etheric body created by our unique electromagnetic fields. Others feel it is a manifestation of various degrees of energy which can be seen as auras of color and intensity. Another group thinks it may be heat emanations from the metabolism of our cells.

Whatever the explanation, there is one thing that can be agreed upon. Every individual on this planet has a comfort zone around their body. Not only does personal space have cultural, family training, and situational factors, it also has a relationship to the quality and quantity of sleep obtained the night before, what's been eaten, and what feelings are held about personal physique as well as an individual's state of emotional, mental, and spiritual being.

Reiki is non-threatening.

The width of these spaces has been documented by thermal sensitive machines and energy detectors. Sensitive people have been known to train themselves to feel these 'spaces' around others' bodies. Changes in these fields have been noted. It has been discovered that arguments tend to increase the need for depth and width of personal space. The decision to be intimate decreases or thins it.

Communication studies claim that interpersonal relationships can be enhanced when attention is paid to individual comfort zones.

My further study of this manifestation, especially with mild to moderately ill patients has increased my awareness of just how intrusive, or how welcome, "touch" becomes in the healing process.

Time and sensitivity is needed to understand the relevancy of another person's ability to be touched. Just having a patient or a client make an appointment is not carte blanche permission to place our hands on their body.

I like the Usui System of Natural Healing, even more now because I realize it is one of the least threatening bodywork techniques. It does not require the client to become naked and exposed. Layers of blankets can be used if an individual so desires. Reiki goes through them.

Reiki also employs a pattern that does not overwhelmingly invade an individual's comfort zone.

Reiki is loving touch. The first head position is the first touch position in a session, and is the least invasive of all touches. Remember the traditionally dramatized comfort of a mother's touch? Most often it is a stroke across the brow of her child. An initial lover's touch usually involves a hand upon a face. A kiss on the forehead can be the first contact of intimacy. Reiki is employed in a similar approach.

Starting a session at the head and over the eyes and brow begins relaxation of the mental body and softens thoughts, perceptions, and personal issues. This 'beginning' reduces anxiety and invites relaxation, the primary need of an over-stressed body. I like to call this "putting the mind at ease".

Even though a client may relax initially, it is important to allow for any change of comfort zone while on the table. At any time during a session, a personal alarm system may go off, announcing that some wall or barrier has been breached. This can be recognized by discomfort on a client's face, or twitching that is akin to restlessness. This may signal a disturbance and needs to be addressed by encouraging any client to feel in charge of the session.

Allow them to adjust to their level of comfort and briefly express, if possible, their distress. This encourages them to relax their guard and allows for increased absorption of Reiki. It also involves them in a special way by assisting them to maintain a sense of self. This involvement does not mean they may chatter constantly about their day or their family or their job. This means they can express their discomfort in sound, breath, or words.

Relaxation can increase the absorption of Reiki.

Obtaining permission at the beginning of any session may be formal or informal. We must also become aware of any clues an individual may give us regarding their hesitancy to get on the table face up or to begin a session that is foreign to their experience.

If reluctance is present, we can offer to place our hands on an area that is causing them discomfort and demonstrate the sensation of warmth or vibration that can occur when we touch an individual's area of need. If they still seem uncomfortable, question them about their reasons for coming or suggest that another time may be better.

The more acknowledgment we give our client's right to their body and their space, the more often we will be given permission to touch and offer Reiki for their benefit.

After the Emergency

We can use Reiki in emergency situations to staunch the flow of blood, to retard the destruction of tissue from a burn, and to keep swelling to a minimum. We can offer our hands to those in an acute respiratory crisis, to assist in the reduction of pain, or to calm anxiety until medical assistance arrives.

Reiki can respond to crisis.

Application of Reiki can be focused on all acute symptoms except a broken bone until it is set in place.[1] After any emergency, to promote health and balance to the entire system that has been traumatized, a total body session is suggested.

Our arms and legs are not independent appendages of our hearts or lungs. Every component of our cardiac, circulatory, respiratory, lymphatic, enzymatic, etc., systems are tied into each other and when one part becomes injured, this entire complex does not just go on standby, it goes into action.

The energy depletion of our body's systems and the toxic waste that is produced after it has been on emergency duty can create further damage

---

[1] Some anecdotes reveal cases where bones have reset themselves during a Reiki application.

to its intricate balance.

Sometimes it is not convenient to stand by the side of a hospital bed for a structured session. Sometimes all that can be managed is a reassuring touch and calm word. This is where Reiki's ability to be transferred from cell to cell assists us. We can hold a hand or a foot and know that, in a space of time, the entire body will receive the energy boost it needs to accomplish its healing.

If time is available, it is always wise to follow-up an emergency problem with a full session. If it's not possible, what we have done is put to use, in the best way possible, what we have at hand.

Intuition

Recently I was asked if there is another way in which to perform the Usui System. This individual had been working with Reiki for many years and, whereas he accepted the value of doing the total session of precise hand positions, he felt he had been drawn to touch other areas that had not been covered in the formalized session.

I have two reactions. Both are supported by personal observations.

The first relies heavily on Takata's teachings that dictate:

"Put the major organs in balance and energize them, and healing will happen."

This is a good practice because often, when a client comes with a specific ailment or symptom, the entire body is out of balance.

In my experience, accomplishing the entire hands-on session will reduce or eliminate the specific complaint by the end of the session. There are times when I will add positions after having completed the head and front sections. My decision to do so is based on my second reaction regarding how to do a full-body session.

I have observed that my hands, simply speaking, take over.

If I can accept the fact that Reiki is pulled through my body in a degree proportionate to the need that is under my hand and I can test that out time and time again on myself and others, then I can come to accept the fact that this energy responds to need.

Basic hand positions are enhanced by intuitively placed hands.

When my hands are in the air as I'm talking, I do not usually have a sensation of pulsation or vibration or heat or coolness. If I place my hand on the telephone receiver or the table or some other object that does not have an identifiable hurt or imbalance, my hand remains "my hand'.

It's when I get around a plant or animal or human being who has an ache or a stress or strain. When I place my hand there, it becomes something more. It has a different feel to it. I perceive it as becoming fuller, or itching, or vibrating, etc.

After many years of this, I've realized that my hands are drawn to a specific place or pain or stress. It's as if the potential energy through my hands is searching for a way to express itself, searching out a need to fill.

How many times have many of us heard, "How did you know I hurt there?" or "My goodness, I didn't know I was so tense until you touched me!"

I repeat, it is not as if I consciously decided to place my hand on a particular spot. My hand was moved there and a connection was made. I am becoming convinced that this is a by-product of the non-judgmental, non-expectation-oriented practice of Reiki. A level of intuition is developed that goes beyond what the mind perceives.

It is this occurrence, I believe, that may also move this system away from a practice that is easily documentable. It could very well be the reason that some health providers and practitioners won't authenticate Reiki. When they ask, "How does it work?" or "Why did you do that?"; the answer comes, "I'm not sure," or "I don't know," or "I just do it and it works."

Doing the basic treatment relieves guess-work.

My only suggestion is one of caution. If when we do the structured approach and we "feel" our hands being drawn to a different position on our client's body, we can follow this pull and do so. We will be able to verify if there is a need in this alternative area by the way our hands react. When the 'draw' is over, then is the time to move on to the next structured hand position, or we can choose to move with the sense of our hands. It is best, however, to be certain that all the usual positions are covered by the end of the session.

We will then be able to document for ourselves the wonder of following the intuition of our hands and still be able to accomplish a routine application of Reiki.

The Final Question

To see you pale and hairless
        In pain, with tiny pupils
To hear your whispered voice ask
        no longer, "Why?" but "When?"
    I feel the pressure build
        behind my eyes
            And around my heart.

To sit and breathe with you,
To wonder, indeed, which breath
        will be your last,
    I feel my throat tighten with
        a flood of unspoken words
            and of unshed tears.

To know there may not be
        many tomorrows.
That all there is
        may be this moment
            of watching with you
            of waiting with you
        for the start of your
            next adventure,
    I find myself holding my breath
        then sighing a prayer
            that your question
                will soon be answered.

                For Sue, 1989
        Excerpted from "Attitudes of Dying"

Hospice

Sometimes the ultimate healing decision is to let loose of this life experience. This occurrence for any practitioner of any healing modality or medical providership challenges the very existence of our practice and beliefs.

All too often, we can get ourselves into an over-focused attitude of wanting each of our clients to attain health in a way that embraces life as we know it.

Reiki can assist in the act of letting go.

Many different sensations can begin to occur for a Reiki Practitioner during a session with a client who is at the 'end stages' of life. Many times our hands can feel pulled into a particular area and we can begin sweating because there is such an intense draw. Sometimes our hands can feel as if they've done nothing but move from one position to another. On many occasions, I've witnessed no particular draw but have noticed an increased relaxation and overall pain reduction in my client. This experience of seemingly 'no' or 'general' draw on hospice clients has brought me to the following understanding.

When, on a personal level, an individual makes the decision to embrace the other side of life, in most cases, the need for Reiki, Universal Life Energy, no longer exists. The cells and tissues of the body have no need to be energized. They are relinquishing their duties, so to speak, as are all the functions of the body, and they are shutting down. It is the way that death of the body occurs.

Even if the person is saying they want to live, somehow, on some level, a decision has been made to pass on to whatever they believe is next. Sometimes, when following the hands-on technique, parts of the body will continue to accept energy and other parts will not.

Hospice work challenges all personal values.

This, of course, isn't a hard and fast rule. There are, in the course of a session, many times when an individual has so much armoring in a particular place, there is a block to the draw of energy from our hands. Sometimes these areas eventually accept Reiki during the session. Individuals who are experiencing a life-threatening illness and who have this armoring, I have discovered, open only minimally to this energy and then only to areas of emotional pain and mental anquish which are around the heart, front and back, and on all head positions. I believe that this is a sign that a client is making peace with themselves and reaching for the ultimate healing.

Working with hospice patients who have all kinds of illnesses is an experience not just in dealing with death and dying, but in dealing with life. Our personal values can be challenged and our understanding of the quality of life can be enriched. Reiki is always there to help.

In one reported case in the AIDS Outreach Program, a young man was living in an isolation room on a hospital ward in Seattle, Washington. He was considered obnoxious and demanding. Few nurses would 'gown up' to enter his room even though they knew he was fearful and anxious.

A friend recommended Reiki Outreach which he initially rejected. The Reiki volunteer persevered, however, put on the required gown, hat, shoes, and gloves, and performed the total body session in his hospital room.

Reiki's continuing gift is the reduction of anxiety in all situations.

With just one session, the young man was able to release a large percentage of his hostility and aggression and become less anxious. Perhaps it was the fact that someone voluntarily took the time to enter his room and touch him in a nonjudgmental fashion. Perhaps it was also the fact that his need for attention was met by the transference of Reiki. In any event, it is reported that with each Reiki session he changed.

Before he passed on, he was able to relate in a more rewarding manner for himself and the staff. His was a room where someone was always stopping in even if they had to go through the process of gowning and ungowning. Reiki helped him change and to pass on with less fear and anxiety.

Even before Hospice Palliative Care is prescribed, Reiki can help. For those experiencing chemotherapy, Reiki can reduce the side effects so therapy can be tolerated to a greater degree. When radiation is prescribed, Reiki assists surrounding tissues to resist breakdown. Post-surgical healing is enhanced with Reiki. Anxiety is reduced so communication regarding difficult personal subjects can be accomplished.

Reiki can reduce the degree of all side effects.

Reiki is a very supportive method for family members during terminal care of their loved ones. Reiki is also very beneficial to Hospice Volunteers. In that it can ease their own anxieties.

My most difficult case of Hospice work was when I attended to the last days of a terminally-ill patient who happened to be a very dear friend. She spoke of her desire to move on to her next adventure and asked continually how she could let go of this life.

I was frustrated and sad because the heat from my hands caused her such discomfort that she was reduced to tears. I couldn't bring my hand more than two feet away from her body. I now believe the cells of her body wanted Reiki but that she had made up her mind to move on and this rejection of the energy was her way of ensuring that it would happen. I learned to sit near her with my hands on my chest or heart to calm myself so I could be there for her in the best way I knew how. I could take care of my pain of losing her and still be present and centered. I could both cry when it was appropriate and help others who came to assist or visit her.

Working with patients who are dying is not for everyone but experiencing death in others will occur to each of us. However we are called upon to serve, our Reiki hands are always with us.

Alternative vs. Complementary

We've come a long way from the horse and buggy days of medicine, when the black bag-carrying doctor knew his patients from birth to death as well as their previous family history. New findings and research results are being announced weekly. New diagnostic tools are created yearly. In order for a doctor to know as much as possible about any segment of medicine, he/she is almost required to specialize.

Allopathic medicine serves best in times of war.

Unfortunately, because we are also a mobile society, many doctors are even farther removed from having a past history available on each patient. To study and treat symptoms only is then an outgrowth of medical specialization and societal transience.

When the concept of viewing each patient as a totality reappeared and became established under the title of Holistic (or Wholistic) Medicine, there was hope that people could find a medical provider who would address an illness with attention to an individual's myriad inter-relationships.

Now there is a full field of Holistic practitioners. There are Iridologists, Reflexologists, Colonic Therapists, Rebirthers, Energy Workers, Massage Therapists, Jin Shin Do Therapists,

Hypnotherapists, Color or Art and Music Therapists. The list goes on and on with all kinds of methods and manners of healing work.

What has developed over the years is another group of specialists, designated as Alternative Therapies or Alternative Medicine.

Somehow, looking at the total patient has become divided and specialized again and according to the definition of the word, alternative, we have become "the other choice."

Holisitic Medicine serves by supporting overall health.

Allopathic and Holistic Medicine can work together. I can speak from experience.

Over a period of four years, I tried several types of "alternative" therapies to reduce my uterine fibroids. I took Vitamin A therapy, was on a vegetarian diet, used visualization, did counseling and hypnotherapy, worked with crystals, attended American Indian Healing Ceremonies, and constantly performed Reiki on myself. The fibroids reduced then returned. I then reviewed issues regarding my femaleness, guilt, shame, anger, and frustration. The fibroids diminished then returned again. I was at the end of my rope.

At the urging of a fellow nurse, I realized I had done a lot of healing work on myself but that I wasn't yet a magician. I needed help to remove the growths, so I went to a Gynecologist and had a hysterectomy. I then used all the skills I had learned so as to return to an improved level of energy and activity. I needed that operation, and I needed all the techniques I had learned to obtain the healing I desired. I came together as the person I am today because I combined therapies. I know they can come together for others.

Holistic Medicine, then, in my present understanding, can stand for both Allopathic and Alternative Methods. It is an attitudinal approach to health care because it treats each case of accident or disease as a total experience of the individual.

X-ray can be combined with Hypnotherapeutic Counseling. Pain medicine can be enhanced with hands-on energy transfer. Chemotherapy can be potentiated by Guided Imagery. Surgery and muscle rehabilitation can be improved with Physical and Music Therapy. All the methods can co-operate. They can complement each other.

Look at Webster's definition of Complementary:

> *"That which completes or makes perfect.....the quantity or amount which when added completes a whole; either of two parts or things needed to complete each other.*

Perhaps we can work toward redefining all procedures, therapies, and health support systems under the title of Complementary Therapies so that each individual can have a grand scope of possibilities available for his/her decision-making process regarding health and healing.

That truly would be Total Health Care, or TLC (Total Life Care).

Responsible Reiki

I became especially concerned recently when I heard of a Reiki practitioner who told a client, "Don't go to see your doctor for two weeks while we're doing Reiki." This request was made of a woman who had been diagnosed as having an ovarian cyst that was possibly malignant. A two week delay can be life-threatening in ovarian cancer and this kind of request, whether or not the cyst disappears, places the client, the practitioner, and Reiki in jeopardy.

In another recent case, a man with glaucoma was told that one session with Reiki could cure his condition. Whether or not this occurs, the statement alone puts all involved in a potentially hazardous position.

A person's healing may not be as we expect.

We can have no idea how or what any body will become as we nurture it.

For example, when I was working in ICU, I cared for a teenage girl who had fallen from a horse onto a pitchfork which had penetrated her brain and left her paralyzed and comatose. At the head of her bed were pictures of what she had been; long hair, bright eyes, wide-open smile. I know they were placed there to give us nurses in ICU an opportunity to focus on who she was as a person rather than the unresponsive body on the bed, attached to the respirator.

.	I also know the trick it played on all our minds. After three months the young girl rolled out of the hospital in her wheelchair still partially paralyzed with slurred speech. Our ICU Head Nurse came back from the girl's send-off in tears because she couldn't help but compare the youngster, at the time of discharge, to the active, capable young person she had appeared to be in the pictures before the accident.

We may not dictate what healing should be for another.

Healing had occurred but she had survived in a different form than hoped for, leaving us with a sense of failure.

It is also true that whenever I try to picture a friend or a patient/client well or whole, my mind moves most often to a picture that is previous to the present.

The pictures of the young girl as well as those I've held in my mind of a sick friend limits their possibilities and sets a case for disappointment.

So does any element of expectation in "making someone whole." We cannot know what that wholeness is. The person we are working with rarely has a clear understanding for their own personal wholeness.

I am not saying that hope is to be denied, only that we must take care in all areas of health treatment and support therapies to relinquish any expectation of a specific result.

We can be ready for change. We cannot predict what that change will be. We also may not dictate what that change must be for anyone.

It is true that miraculous changes have been recorded with the use of Reiki. However, it is the setting up for the expectation of those changes that is most often a need of the practitioner to plan or control the outcome. This is inappropriate and detrimental to the practice of Reiki. It predisposes us to failure as an acceptable part of the team for health and health care.

I only promise that Reiki will bring about change.

We must use our system with care and responsibility. We must forego the temptation to "make things right," to place our egos on the line and to pretend we know what the outcome of any Reiki session may be.

I have come to the place now, that all I promise is that something will change, or that a change will occur. I leave it up to the individual to be sensitive to his/her body so as to be aware of whatever that change is. I only promise that for Reiki to work, it has to be used. I am taking the guesswork out of the results of a session, because I make no guesses.

Note also that I say "session". In my mind, at this time, because we are not legally allowed to treat anyone, I have changed my approach to stating that I have Reiki sessions, or hands-on sessions. I also have a Disclaimer for signing at each session. **I encourage individuals to see their doctor on a regular basis, to continue to have their condition and health monitored, and never to stop taking any medication unless they check with their doctor first.**

When changes occur in people who come to

me for sessions, I ask if they would be willing to help me document those changes. This can ultimately assist the Usui System of Natural Healing to collect accurate and thorough observations for the medical community.

I believe that I am not only protecting myself, I believe I am protecting Reiki by not putting it out on a limb. Reiki is too important to allow it to become challenged unnecessarily.

Mantra

My soul cries for enough space

       within which to roam

  But also enough limits

       by which to be guided.

My soul prays for enough silence

       within which to find peace,

  But also enough words

       by which to express itself.

My soul seeks enough aloneness

       in which to develop

  And enough touching

       by which to announce its

       presence.

efg;1978

83

For the Future

Did you know that Reiki is being taught in Virginia as Healing Hands and that the Radiance Technique, as well as Radiant Reiki, Mari-El and the Teachings of the Cauldron of Thoth have their origins in the Usui System of Natural Healing?

Reiki has seen many changes to its basic form.

There is now also an "Usui Lightworks" as well as a Master's Symbol fashioned out of magnetized metal and plastic, and a reworked version of our teachings named Omega.

Another Reiki group offers First and Second Degree Classes on the same weekend, and a third organization initiates interested students to all three levels over three days. There is a system that has 'seven degrees' of Reiki.

There are as many variations and interpretations of Reiki being taught now as there are individuals to teach. This has brought conflict, anger, and jealousy.

These reactions create confusion and doubt in the minds of other body workers and medical professionals as to any documentable cause and effect of Reiki. The various changes and our various reactions also undermine our credibility.

I find I'm frustrated by these changes and reactions. How can Reiki become validated enough to be addressed with any kind of seriousness by the medical profession so that we can somehow begin to work together?

The only way I can begin to understand why there are so many methods is to return to my own experience.

When I first began practicing the Usui System, I felt I was on the crest of a wave. My perceptions were heightened. I was personally convinced that Reiki was the answer to humankind. I still believe this but in the context that any connection with Universal Life Energy, however a person wants to name it and in whatever form or system he or she wants to practice it, can be transformational.

Astounding changes in personal perception can occur with Reiki.

Through the Usui System, I feel I've experienced an opening of my inner voice and developed an increased capacity to hear. In the beginning, I was enthralled when my mind and hands were guided to places on a person's body, and I sensed messages regarding the sensations in my hands. I started hearing voices which urged me to say certain things to my clients or to have them picture certain colors under my hands. I received ideas about how to assist a client to look into a past life or lives for information regarding their infirmities.

As a part of my growing interested in all healing modalities, I began reading more about Color Therapy, Light Therapy, and Hypnosis. I had already taken classes in Aura Reading, Guided Imagery, Peer-Crisis Counseling, Chakra Balancing.

I began to sense myself in a kind of frenzy, to do all, to be all, encompass all. I saw everything as it seemed to fit together but I couldn't bring it all together.

I had also added so much to my practice of Reiki, I had overlaid the basic gift of balance and re-energizing by adding other methods and techniques. Because Reiki is so simple, I had decided that Reiki needed to be more, but I had made it so complicated that my clients had become more dependent on me, not less.

Reiki remains a simple tool. It's you and I who try to embellish

When I brought my heightened perceptions and visions to my clients, they were grateful for the information, but in the end, I felt much as Usui must have felt in his story with the beggars in the slums of Tokyo. The changes I had expected and envisioned in these clients were not forthcoming. They were my expectations and visions, not theirs. I was in essence telling them their process rather than allowing them to live it on their own.

This is what I believe is happening in the vast arena of New Age developments and with Reiki.

Each individual has had an awakening to the energy, to the light, to what is beyond this earth plane. Because we are each unique prisms of light from the Creator, of the Goddess Mother, or the Great Spirit, or Buddha, (whichever system of belief you subscribe to...) we each have our set of perspectives on this life and our individually de-signed set of skills and gifts. The awakening that happens for each of us, when we are ready to allow it to occur, brings us into contact with all the possibilities and, most importantly, our individual uniqueness. The energy, being universal, touches those gifts and makes them part of our growth as well as part of the way we express ourselves to the world in which we relate.

The many different classes and methods that have been developed are being created in response to the instructor's individual awakening. He or she is offering their awareness and self-discovery as a new method. It works for them; it can work for everyone.

Every Reiki student has their own unique lessons.

It is here that a big problem occurs, as I see it. A bit of ego gets in the way. The self-discovery no longer becomes "my way"; it becomes "The Way", because each ego wants to share it, often for profit.

Often it is a case of a teacher or a guru or a Master teaching their own personal process and discovery as something which is supposed to happen next. This removes from students their responsibility to practice Reiki and experience their own awakening as well as their own truths through their own unique skills and gifts.

We each have our own lessons.

Thus, I only teach the Usui System of Natural Healing, and I teach it as closely as possible to the traditional mode. I use tapes of Ms. Takata speaking and of my Master, Fran Brown teaching to keep me on track. I want to leave each student open to his or her own growth pattern. Reiki is a new beginning, not the middle, and never the end.

It adds and expands each of our worlds so that we may be healthier and more able to stand as unique individuals.

These many Reiki methods are only the natural outgrowths of a successful system. For we are not the only system that changed by personal vision or "divine" guidance. History shows religions have splintered and new denominations have developed. Medical Science splits itself apart with every new specialty developed and recognized. In the Holistic Arena, new energy therapies or bodywork movements are designed constantly.

The challenge for each new stream of Reiki is to maintain a standard of integrity in its application of this universal energy. This can create a basic form of consensus so that Reiki sessions and their results can be documented. If a stream of Reiki cannot participate in this agreement, then I suggest the creator develop another name by which to call what they have created.

Because we are truly on the verge of changing our world, we need as many enlightened and loving people as can emerge. We need as many methods as there are individuals so that something will speak to everyone. Agreeing to come together in at least the method of application is the beginning of establishing an ethical guide of Reiki practice and purpose.

The continuation of life on this planet in a healthy way and within a healthy environment requires our attitudes encompass all possibilities. We can, however, monitor ourselves responsibly, while continuing to offer ourselves and our gifts to all.

Trust Reiki

With all the Reiki books on the market these days, as well as other energy healing techniques, plus hundreds of self-help books, a student can read from dawn to dusk. I am concerned about this trend even though I know I've added my own two cents to the printed world.

I've lived with Reiki now for over 18 years. There were no books to read in the beginning, and I feel fortunate in that fact. To learn about Reiki, I had to do it. There was no other way. I placed my hands either on myself or on a member of my family or a friend. I chattered on and on about Reiki to anyone who would listen and was generally a pest about the topic.

Reading about Reiki does not replace doing it.

When I stepped into the role of Reiki Master in 1988, I began by teaching anyone who was interested, and then, I developed a class for registered nurses. The objectives for this nurses' continuing education class had to be listed as specific skills to expand, for the nurse, the practice of caring for patients. For this reason, my class took on a clinical tone. I felt I was limiting their experience. Because I wanted them to have the details of other aspects of Reiki, this book was born.

It was never meant to usurp the experience of First Degree training but to add to it.

Now, most students who come to classes have read at least one and sometimes five books on Reiki. They are also involved with some other form of energy healing, such as massage, aromatherapy, etc. and are interested in learning yet another 'form'.

After the class, I find they are reading yet more books on Reiki, or on the value of 21 day meditations for empowerment or abundance, or reading on how gemstones can be included as well as tonal therapy, and the list can go on and on.

They remind me of my relationship to the computer. I am excited to have this new tool for self-expression. I regularly try to learn something new by reading help files. I can read the help files for hours, but it's not until I pull down a file, make a choice, and push the apply button that I truly experience the capacity of the computer. Reading about Reiki is like storing knowledge. It is not until one places one's hands on self or another that the energy becomes real and the potential of change becomes imminent.

All that is not Reiki can be released with personal use.

I also hear confusion regarding what a student feels they need to do next in their life or questions regarding their relationship with themselves, their family, their world, and their spiritual life. These questions I believe can be answered as an individual settles into the practice of Reiki itself. Spending time with self-treatment, after first asking one specific question regarding next right action, or standing quietly to offer Reiki to a friend or family member, brings about the very same relaxed state of consciousness which can support an opportunity to gain centeredness and balance.

Reading a book about Reiki does not bring about the same kind of relaxation and opportunity for focus as doing Reiki.

For this reason, I recommend that students spend the first three months after their First Degree class in complete isolation from reading about Reiki. I ask them to make the commitment to doing Reiki instead. I ask them to wait and see what comes up, what surfaces for them to do, what changing situation or attitude is unfolding for them, and I ask them to trust Reiki.

This hiatus from the input of books and other people's experiences can be instituted at any time. Once the decision is made, then the attention can be to building a relationship with Reiki through self and other treatment.

Treat yourself to a timeout from reading about Reiki and just do it!

Whether this time is directly after a First Degree class or two or more years later, I hope that students will take the pause to allow universal energy to work for them. This thrill of self-discovery is part of an exciting Reiki experience and a reward for having made a step into another level of possibility. What is to be known and experienced will be perfect because it will be filtered through an individual's natural abilities and prior experiences. No one else can experience Reiki in exactly the same way; no one can describe the possibilities that are to be available when an individual trusts themselves and this potential they now embody.

The Challenge

There are many methods by which to channel energy. The Usui System of Natural Healing is but one. There are many ways of saying energy. Reiki is the name I use, along with thousands of others.

You may wish to learn another method or incorporate many techniques to create your own unique style. Whatever you are guided to do, please know, that at this time, you have allowed yourself the gift of healing energy and it is in your hands.

It's simple. It is also enough.

It's now up to you......

REIKI

WILL ONLY WORK

IF

YOU USE IT!

About the Author

Earlene Gleisner lives with her husband in a small community in Northern California. She works as an RN at a rural health center, manages White Feather Press, and teaches the Usui System of Natural Healing. She travels to wherever there are interested students and provides CE credit for RNs in California. She offers several experiential seminars: "Deepening Your Experience With Reiki", based on the Five Precepts, "Talking To A Stone", an opportunity for developing personal ritual and reconnecting with the Earth, and "Writing for a Change", a creative experience with focus.

In 2002, she contributed a chapter on "Reiki" in the Principles and Practice of Manual Therapeutics, A Medical Guide to Complementary and Alternative Medicine published by Churchill/Livingstone. Reiki As A Complementary Therapy demonstrates scientific and practical evidence of Reiki. A short fiction, Just For Today, presents a teaching on the Principles of Reiki with a Native American flavor. Other fiction and non-fiction books are in process.

Her books and classes have been developed to follow her life's work of encouraging others to embrace their connection and relationship to themselves and each other, to their natural world and their spiritual path. Anyone interested in further information can reach her through White Feather Press, POB 1209, Laytonville, CA, 95454-1209 or current email: reiki@mcn.org.

About The Cover: Robert Howard Graphic Design of Ft. Collins, CO. created the professional design which is based on photographs by Bob Yuwach Gleisner. The center flower is a day lily which blooms brilliantly and fully for one day and was chosen to remind us to pay attention to the preciousness of each moment.

Ordering Information

Reiki in Everyday Living

_____ * First Edition   ($12.95)   _____
_____ * Second Edition ($13.95)   _____
_____ **Just for Today** ($5.00)   _____
_____ Reiki As A Complementary Therapy
            ($10.00 for a xerox copy)   _____
_____ **In the Light of a Distant Star**
            by Wanja Twan ($18.00)   _____
*Available on Amazon.com

So as to focus on the beauty of the Reiki symbol, White Feather Press has made available fine silver jewelry in the form of a pendant, earrings, or lapel and scarf pin.

霊
気
Reiki

_____ Pendant ($20)   _____

_____ Earrings ($36)

            on French Wire   _____

            on Posts   _____

_____ Lapel Pin ($20)   _____

SHIPPING: _____
Book Rate ($3.50) First Class ($5.50)
Jewelry First Class ($3.50 per six units of jewelry)
CA sales tax is .0750   _____
(Wholesale terms available)
GRAND TOTAL   _____
MAIL TO:

white feather press

P.O. BOX 1209   /   43055 HIGHWAY 101 N.
LAYTONVILLE, CA 95454   (707) 984-6048